A BUSINESS APPROACH TO PINEAPPLE FARMING

Complete Entrepreneurial Step By Step Guide To Pineapple Garden From Scratch

ZHURI HART

DISCLAIMER

This book is intended to provide general information and insights on adopting a business approach to farming. The content within is based on the author's knowledge and experiences up to the date of publication. It is essential to recognize that the field of agriculture is dynamic, influenced by various factors such as market conditions, climate, and regulatory changes.

Readers are advised to conduct thorough research, seek professional advice, and consider their unique circumstances before implementing any strategies or practices discussed in this book. The author and publisher disclaim any responsibility for the accuracy, completeness, or suitability of the information provided. The book is not a substitute for professional advice, and the author and publisher shall not be liable for any damages or losses arising from the use or reliance on the information presented herein.

Individual results may vary, and success in farming enterprises is contingent upon numerous variables. The author encourages readers to consult with relevant experts, agricultural extension services, and legal or financial professionals to tailor strategies to their specific needs and local conditions.

This book is not intended to be a comprehensive guide to all aspects of farming, and readers should exercise their judgment and discretion in applying the principles discussed. The author and publisher do not endorse any specific products, services, or companies mentioned in this book unless explicitly stated.

By reading this book, the reader acknowledges and accepts the inherent uncertainties in agricultural endeavors and agrees to use the information at their own risk.

TABLE OF CONTENTS

ABOUT THE BOOK

"A Business Approach to Pineapple Farming" is a priceless manual for anyone hoping to get into the pineapple farming business or improve their current operations. The background and importance of pineapple farming as a business are thoroughly explored at the beginning of the book, laying the groundwork for the in-depth insights that follow.

The book go into great length into the complexities of pineapple growing, including a botanical review, a description of the varieties and their traits, and a summary of the necessary soil and climate conditions. This information serves as the foundation for the sections that follow, which walk readers through the painstaking planning and design of a pineapple plantation.

The importance placed on business planning in the book is one of its main features. By delving deeply into feasibility studies, creating business plans, budgeting, and financial predictions, readers gain the knowledge and skills necessary to make wise choices in the cutthroat world of pineapple farming. Resilience against future obstacles is further ensured by the integration of risk management solutions.

Beyond just the theoretical, the book provides helpful advice on starting and running farms. The topics of land preparation, planting methods, irrigation systems, and thorough pest and disease control procedures are all covered, offering a comprehensive strategy for productive and sustainable pineapple farming.

With sections devoted to organic pineapple farming, integrated pest control, water conservation strategies, and the advancement of biodiversity and ecosystem services, sustainability is still a recurrent theme. This indicates how ecologically friendly farming methods are becoming more and more important in contemporary agriculture.

A thorough discussion of harvesting and post-harvest handling is provided, including measures for quality control, maturity assessment, and harvesting processes.

To guarantee that the item reaches the market in the best possible shape, these insights are priceless.

The book's final section focuses on sales and marketing tactics. Through an examination of distribution methods, a focus on branding and packaging, an awareness of market trends, and the creation of potent sales tactics, readers acquire a thorough grasp of how to place their pineapple products in a cutthroat market.

The book also discusses certification schemes, environmental and social responsibility, and regulatory compliance, giving readers a comprehensive understanding of the moral and legal issues involved in pineapple cultivation.

The book examines growing markets, environmental innovations, and technological advancements as potential future trends in pineapple farming. By taking a forward-looking stance, the authors make sure that readers are ready for both the current state of the pineapple farming sector and its future developments.

"A Business Approach to Pineapple Farming" is essentially more than just a manual; it's a tactical ally for those who are dedicated to creating profitable and long-lasting pineapple farming operations. The book equips readers with the information and resources they need to successfully negotiate the difficulties of the pineapple farming industry through its well-organized and thorough material.

CHAPTER ONE

PINEAPPLE FARMING INTRODUCTION

CONTEXT AND IMPORTANCE

A prominent place in the agricultural landscape is occupied by pineapple farming, which is distinguished by its tropical beginnings and global cultivation. Pineapple agriculture has a long history, dating back centuries, and its roots may be found in South America, specifically in the countries of Paraguay and southern Brazil. From its modest origins, pineapple has developed into a widely consumed fruit with a wide range of uses in the industrial, culinary, and medical domains. Its distinct flavor profile and adaptability make it a mainstay in numerous cuisines, which adds to its widespread appeal.

Beyond its culinary uses, pineapple farming is significant because it is essential to the economic growth of the areas where it is grown. Many farmers and towns depend on pineapple growing for their living, which boosts rural economies and creates job possibilities. In addition, pineapple exports have grown to be a profitable industry for many nations, promoting global trade and economic expansion.

Growing pineapples is not without its difficulties because the crop is prone to several illnesses and climatic conditions that might reduce harvests. To overcome these obstacles and guarantee the sustainability of pineapple farming, technological and agricultural advancements have become essential. Thus, pineapple farming is important not just for its economic contributions but also for its ability to adapt and persevere in the face of complicated agricultural challenges.

AN OVERVIEW OF THE BUSINESS OF PINEAPPLE FARMING

From the perspective of a business endeavor, pineapple farming includes a wide range of activities, from marketing to agriculture. A thorough grasp of the crop's life cycle, ideal growth conditions, and post-harvest procedures is necessary for successful pineapple farming. To increase yields and quality, pineapple farmers frequently invest in contemporary agricultural techniques, such as effective irrigation systems, insect control strategies, and soil management techniques.

The potential for profitability of pineapple farming, both locally and globally, emphasizes its business side. Farmers and entrepreneurs alike understand the importance of producing a product that has a steady and expanding market demand. The stability and profitability of pineapple farming businesses are facilitated by the tropical fruit's widespread appeal around the world and its use in a variety of culinary dishes.

Trade laws, consumer preferences, and market dynamics are all essential to the pineapple farming industry. Farmers must have a thorough understanding of these elements to choose crop varieties, output levels, and marketing tactics. Furthermore, the way pineapple farming companies are positioned in the international market is increasingly influenced by sustainability measures and adherence to ethical farming standards.

Pineapple farming as a company emphasizes its diverse character by fusing conventional farming methods with cutting-edge methods and business plans. In addition to the growing of tropical fruit, the success of pineapple farming endeavors depends on farmers' capacity to handle the intricacies of the agricultural sector, adapt to market needs, and support the long-term growth of their local communities.

CHAPTER TWO

COMPREHENDING THE PRACTICE OF PINEAPPLE FARMING

AN OVERVIEW OF PINEAPPLE BOTANY

Ananas comosus, the scientific name for pineapple, is a member of the Bromeliaceae family. Originating in South America, this tropical fruit is currently grown all over the world. The plant is characterized by its long, sword-shaped leaves that are grouped in a rosette arrangement.

It often reaches a height of four or five feet. The stiff, prickly outer skin and sweet, juicy meat of the pineapple fruit, which grows from the core of the vine, are its defining features.

The botanical structure of pineapple plants, which are categorized as perennial herbaceous plants, is essential to comprehending both their growth and care.

DIFFERENT TYPES OF PINEAPPLES AND THEIR FEATURES

Around the world, many pineapple types are grown, and each has unique qualities. The Smooth Cayenne is the most widely available commercial type, distinguished by its big size, golden-yellow hue, and superb flavor. Queen Victoria, MD-2 (sometimes referred to as Golden Sweet), and Sugarloaf are a few other noteworthy kinds. Each variety satisfies a range of consumer tastes with unique attributes like taste, texture, and size. Climate, market demand, and the variety's intended use—whether it is for fresh consumption or processing into juices and canned goods—are all important considerations for farmers when selecting cultivars.

CONDITIONS OF THE SOIL AND CLIMATE

Soil quality and climate have a big impact on pineapple growth. Tropical and subtropical settings, with temperatures between 65°F and 95°F (18°C and 35°C), are ideal for pineapple growth. They cannot tolerate extremely low temperatures and are vulnerable to frost. For pineapple farming, 50 to 100 inches of yearly rainfall that is evenly spread throughout the year is optimal. Sandy-loam soils that drain well and have a pH range of slightly acidic to neutral are thought to be ideal for growing pineapples. Pineapple plants need full sun for the majority of the day to grow and thrive, thus they must receive enough sunshine.

ORGANIZING THE PINEAPPLE FARM'S DESIGN

A pineapple farm's ability to succeed mostly depends on its ability to plan and design efficiently. Considerations including land selection, layout, and spacing need to be made before starting a pineapple farm. It is important to provide pineapple plants enough room to breathe and receive sunlight. Planting in rows or blocks can be chosen as a layout according to the geography and size of the particular farm. To stop soil erosion on sloping terrain, contour planting is also advised. In regions that receive a lot of rainfall, farmers frequently use raised beds or ridges to improve drainage.

In addition, it is imperative to strategically employ irrigation systems to guarantee stable moisture levels, particularly in arid regions. Depending on the size of their farm and the availability of water, farmers can choose between drip irrigation and furrow irrigation. Mulching is another popular technique for preserving soil moisture, inhibiting weed growth, and preserving the ideal soil temperature. Healthy pineapple development requires proper nutrition management, which includes applying fertilizers high in potassium, phosphorus, and nitrogen.

Successful pineapple farming requires a thorough study of the botanical features, cultivars, climate needs, and farm architecture. Growers can maximize pineapple productivity and provide premium fruits for domestic and foreign markets by integrating these factors into the cultivation process.

CHAPTER THREE

PLANNING A BUSINESS

AN ANALYSIS OF THE VIABILITY OF PINEAPPLE FARMING

An important first step in assessing a pineapple farming venture's potential is to conduct a feasibility study. This research entails a thorough evaluation of several variables, including market demand, soil quality, climate, and potential hazards.

To determine whether a piece of land is suitable for growing pineapples, testing on the soil should be conducted, taking into account elements like acidity and nutrient levels. To comprehend consumer preferences, pricing trends, and rivalry within the pineapple business, market research should also be carried out.

The feasibility assessment helps identify potential obstacles that may occur during pineapple cultivation and provides a basis for well-informed decision-making.

CREATING A BUSINESS STRATEGY

Any successful company venture, including growing pineapples, must have a well-written business strategy. The pineapple farm's goals and mission, as well as the target market, production method, and marketing tactics, should all be covered in the business plan.

A schedule for implementation, an organizational chart, and the roles and duties of important team members should also be included. Financial details such as projected revenue, operating costs, and startup costs must be stated in detail.

The business plan is a crucial instrument for drawing investors or obtaining funding since it acts as a road map for the pineapple farming endeavor, giving it direction and consistency.

ESTIMATING FINANCES AND CREATING A BUDGET

A vital component of efficient financial management in pineapple growing is budgeting. It includes projecting and budgeting for the costs related to clearing land, planting, watering, fertilizing, controlling pests, and harvesting. Precise budgeting guarantees the effective distribution of resources, hence reducing the possibility of excessive expenditure.

Contrarily, financial forecasts entail making predictions about future earnings and outlays in light of past performance and industry trends. Projections help with decision-making and enable necessary revisions to the business plan by giving a realistic picture of the farm's financial performance.

Maintaining financial stability and adjusting to shifting market conditions require routinely comparing actual financial performance to projections.

TECHNIQUES FOR RISK MANAGEMENT

Like any agricultural endeavor, growing pineapples is not without danger. These risks include variations in the weather, pests, illnesses, and unstable markets. To reduce these uncertainties, effective risk management techniques must be put into practice. The implementation of sustainable farming methods, insurance coverage, and crop diversification are proactive strategies aimed at reducing the risks connected with climate and market conditions. Systems for integrated pest management can aid in pest control without unduly depending on chemical treatments. For timely intervention, disease monitoring and early identification are essential. Furthermore, forming strategic alliances with vendors and purchasers can act as a cushion against changes in the industry. A strong risk management strategy guarantees sustainability and resilience in the face of unforeseen obstacles, improving the business's overall performance in pineapple cultivation.

CHAPTER FOUR

ESTABLISHMENT AND MANAGEMENT OF FARMS

PLANTING & LAND PREPARATION

Careful planning and thoughtful planting lay the groundwork for a successful farm establishment. Clearing the field of undesired vegetation, rocks, and rubbish is the first step in land preparation. Next, the soil is tilled to enhance its drainage, aeration, and structure. When irrigation is used, even water distribution requires precise field leveling. The crop will determine the best planting technique; in pineapple farms, suckers or crowns are usually used.

When growing pineapples, it is important to take into account the distance between plants to provide sufficient light penetration, airflow, and growing space. The crop's general health is influenced by planting depth and the amount of organic matter incorporated into the soil. To maintain soil moisture inhibit weed growth and create an environment that is conducive to the growth of pineapple plants, farmers can also use mulching techniques.

PINEAPPLE FARM IRRIGATION SYSTEMS

In areas with erratic rainfall patterns, efficient irrigation is essential to a profitable pineapple crop. Several types of irrigation systems can be used, including furrow, sprinkler, and drip irrigation. For pineapple farming, drip irrigation—which supplies water straight to the root zone of the plant—is frequently recommended since it conserves water and lowers the possibility of foliar infections.

Sprinkler systems mimic natural rainfall by providing overhead irrigation. Although this technique guarantees even water distribution, there may be a higher chance of some illnesses. Making channels to move water between the rows of pineapple plants is known as furrow irrigation. Pineapple yields can be adversely affected by water stress or waterlogging, which can be avoided with careful planning and monitoring of irrigation.

MANAGEMENT OF PESTS AND DISEASES

A variety of pests and diseases can seriously impair the health and yield of pineapple crops. Sustainable pest management requires the application of Integrated Pest Management (IPM) techniques. This strategy combines chemical, cultural, and biological control techniques. To organically manage pest populations, beneficial insects might be introduced, such as parasites or predators.

Effective management necessitates early discovery, swift action, and routine pest and disease scouting. To reduce the negative effects on the environment and protect beneficial creatures, chemical control techniques, such as the use of certified pesticides, should be utilized sparingly. Crop rotation is an additional tactic to break up insect life cycles and lessen the accumulation of pathogens in the soil. It entails shifting the locations of crops within a field over time.

CROP ROTATION AND COMPANION PLANTING

To preserve soil fertility, manage pests and diseases, and maximize crop health, crop rotation is an essential management technique in pineapple farms. Pests and soil-borne diseases peculiar to pineapples can be reduced by rotating pineapple with other crops. Furthermore, some crops can improve soil fertility and promote healthier pineapple development by adding particular nutrients to the soil.

To maximize benefits for both parties, companion planting entails planting complementary crops close to pineapples. For instance, some companion plants can naturally support development or deter pests that frequently harm pineapples. Companion planting is successful when the symbiotic interactions between various plants are understood. This all-encompassing method of growing pineapples promotes a healthy ecosystem, which helps pineapple farms remain sustainable over the long term.

CHAPTER FIVE

ECOLOGICAL FARMING METHODS
GROWING PINEAPPLES ORGANICALLY

The holistic approach to agricultural production embraced by organic pineapple farming emphasizes ecosystem health and environmental sustainability. Organic pineapple farming emphasizes natural resources and procedures as opposed to traditional farming techniques, which mostly rely on synthetic chemicals. Instead of employing artificial fertilizers and pesticides, it makes use of organic substitutes including compost, cover crops, and natural predators.

This technique reduces the negative effects on the environment, improves soil health, and yields pineapple crops devoid of hazardous chemical residues. Crop diversification and rotation are also prioritized in organic pineapple farming, which promotes the long-term fertility and resilience of the soil.

MANAGEMENT OF INTEGRATED PESTS (IPM)

An ecologically conscious approach to pest management is called integrated pest management, or IPM. It is a sustainable farming method. Biological, cultural, mechanical, and chemical techniques are all combined in integrated pest management (IPM) to effectively control pest populations. IPM encourages crop rotation, habitat modification, and the use of natural predators in addition to chemical pesticides. Farmers that practice integrated pest management (IPM) can limit environmental damage, lower the use of pesticides overall, and improve ecosystem health by monitoring pest populations and implementing targeted interventions. This method stresses the value of balance and aims to control pests without upsetting the environment's natural equilibrium.

METHODS OF CONSERVING WATER

Sustainable farming practices require the use of water conservation techniques, particularly in areas that are experiencing drought and water scarcity. Farmers use a variety of techniques, like drip irrigation, rainwater collection, and soil moisture management, to maximize the use of water. By delivering water straight to the roots of the plants, drip irrigation reduces water loss from evaporation or runoff. The process of gathering and storing rainwater for use in agriculture during dry spells is known as rainwater harvesting. Techniques like mulching and cover crops, which assist preserve soil moisture and lessen the need for excessive watering, are part of efficient soil moisture management. Farmers can help ensure that water resources are used efficiently and that aquatic ecosystems are preserved by using these water conservation measures.

NATURAL RESOURCES AND ECOSYSTEM SERVICES

Sustainable agricultural methods are fundamentally dependent on biodiversity and ecosystem services.

Retaining biodiversity on and around farms promotes resilience and ecological equilibrium.

By using buffer zones, cover crops, and hedgerows, farmers may promote biodiversity. By establishing homes for beneficial insects, birds, and other wildlife, these methods promote pollination and natural pest management. Furthermore, maintaining natural ecosystems near farms improves the availability of ecosystem services like soil fertility, water purification, and climate management. Acknowledging the interdependence of agriculture and the wider environment, sustainable farming endeavors to augment biodiversity and utilize ecosystem services to establish robust and efficient agricultural systems.

An ethical and ecologically friendly approach to agriculture must include sustainable agricultural methods including organic pineapple farming, integrated pest management, water conservation strategies, and the development of biodiversity and ecosystem services.

CHAPTER SIX

METHODS FOR HARVESTING AND HANDLING PINEAPPLES

AFTER HARVEST

One of the most important factors in a successful pineapple harvest is determining its maturity. Selecting pineapples at the ideal level of maturity is crucial for achieving the best flavor and quality because they do not considerably ripen after harvest.

The color of the fruit is one widely recognized indicator of pineapple maturity. A mature pineapple will usually be bright yellow with very little green, meaning that its sweetness and acidity are just right. Furthermore, the fruit's scent may serve as a trustworthy signal.

A fragrant, sweet scent rises from the base of a ripe pineapple, indicating that it is ready to be harvested.

METHODS OF HARVESTING

Precise and careful harvesting is necessary to maintain the quality of the fruit. One popular method is hand harvesting, in which knowledgeable laborers use a sharp knife to carefully cut the fruit from the plant. This technique makes it possible to harvest pineapples selectively, ensuring that only fully ripe, edible pineapples are gathered. Although less prevalent, machine harvesting can also be used for large-scale operations. To efficiently chop and gather pineapples, specific equipment is used. To minimize post-harvest losses, no fruit damage must occur during the harvesting process, regardless of the method used.

AFTER-HARVEST MANAGEMENT AND PRESERVATION

A key factor in preserving the freshness and caliber of harvested pineapples is post-harvest management. Pineapples are usually washed to get rid of dirt and debris after harvest. After that, fruits are sorted according to size and quality. To increase pineapple shelf life, proper storage is necessary. Common cold storage temperatures are around 10°C (50°F), which slows down the ripening process.

To stop mold and rot, proper ventilation and humidity management are also essential. Fruit damage is significantly reduced and preserved during transit when packaged in corrugated boxes or crates.

MEASURES FOR QUALITY CONTROL

Quality control procedures are carried out in multiple phases, from the field to the ultimate distribution. During harvesting, visual examinations are carried out to guarantee that only pineapples that are visually beautiful and mature are collected. Sorting fruits after harvest aids in removing spoiled or subpar produce.

To stop spoiling, it's crucial to regularly check the temperature and humidity levels during storage. Periodically inspecting the pineapples that are being preserved for potential diseases and pests is another aspect of quality control. Proper labeling and packaging also aid in traceability and support informed customer decision-making. By putting these quality control procedures in place, pineapples of the best possible quality are guaranteed to reach consumers.

CHAPTER SEVEN

STRATEGIES FOR MARKETING AND SALES

RECOGNIZING MARKET TRENDS

Any business hoping to maintain its competitiveness in the ever-changing business world must recognize market trends. Changes in customer behavior, preferences, and industry dynamics are all included in market trends.

Remaining aware of these patterns enables companies to foresee shifts and modify their approaches appropriately. This entails keeping an eye on current trends as well as projecting future advancements.

Businesses can find new possibilities, risks, and areas for innovation by analyzing market trends.

It entails a thorough analysis of economic data, societal changes, technology developments, and customer demographics.

PACKAGING AND BRANDING

An organization's entire marketing plan must include both branding and packaging. Beyond merely a logo, branding embodies a company's values and the commitments it makes to its clientele. Strong branding establishes a unique personality and a sentimental bond with customers. It entails developing an engaging story, outlining key principles, and consistently delivering these components over all touchpoints. Conversely, the brand's physical and visible manifestation is its packaging. It is a potent marketing tool in addition to providing products with protection. Packaging that is visually appealing, practical, and eco-friendly can affect how consumers feel about products and make judgments about what to buy.

CHANNELS OF DISTRIBUTION

Selecting appropriate channels of distribution is a crucial component of a business's marketing and sales plan. The route via which goods or services go to the final customer is known as the distribution channel. It entails choosing whether to sell through intermediaries, direct channels, or a combination of the two. The best distribution strategy depends on several variables, including the product's nature, the target market, and the competitive environment. Distribution channels include things like wholesalers, direct sales, brick-and-mortar stores, and e-commerce websites. Ensuring product availability at the desired location and time for clients is the aim, along with cost minimization and efficiency optimization.

FORMULATING ROBUST SALES APPROACHES:

Creating sales tactics that work demands a comprehensive approach that complements the overarching business goals. Developing compelling value propositions, knowing your target market, and providing salespeople with the right training are all essential components of a winning sales strategy. To effectively position items or services as solutions, sales professionals must possess a thorough awareness of consumer needs and pain spots. Businesses can segment their markets and customize their strategies to target particular client categories by leveraging data-driven insights. Developing enduring relationships with clients is also crucial since they are essential to continued success because they encourage recurring business and customer loyalty. By offering useful statistics and monitoring customer interactions, technology, such as customer relationship management (CRM) systems, can improve the efficacy and efficiency of sales efforts.

CHAPTER EIGHT

CERTIFICATION AND REGULATORY COMPLIANCE

LEGAL CONDITIONS FOR GROWING PINEAPPLES

Like any other agricultural operation, growing pineapples is governed by several laws that are meant to safeguard consumer safety, preserve the environment, and uphold ethical business practices. Adherence to laws about pesticide use, food safety, water management, and land use are examples of these legal requirements. Zoning laws, which determine appropriate sites for agricultural activities while taking into account elements like soil quality and environmental impact, must be followed by farmers who grow pineapples.

Additionally, to prevent environmental contamination and safeguard the health of both customers and farm workers, certain rules govern the use of fertilizers and pesticides in pineapple production.

Agrochemical labeling, storage, and application must often be done correctly to comply with these requirements. Moreover, to prove compliance with these rules when inspected, producers are typically expected to maintain documentation of their farming methods.

CERTIFICATION PROGRAMS

In pineapple farming, certification programs are essential for developing and confirming adherence to industry standards. Farmers can show their dedication to sustainable, high-quality, and ethical farming practices through these voluntary programs. Common certification programs for pineapple farming include organic certification, Fair Trade certification, and various sustainability certifications.

Organic certification ensures that pineapples are grown without synthetic pesticides, herbicides, and genetically modified organisms. This designation is particularly appealing to consumers who prioritize organic and environmentally friendly products. Fair Trade certification, on the other hand, focuses on ethical labor practices and fair wages for workers. Pineapple farms seeking Fair Trade certification must adhere to standards that promote social responsibility and fair treatment of employees.

Sustainability certifications may cover a range of environmental practices, such as water conservation, soil management, and biodiversity preservation. These certifications recognize pineapple farms that implement sustainable farming techniques and minimize their ecological footprint. By participating in certification programs, pineapple farmers not only enhance the marketability of their products but also contribute to the overall improvement of industry standards.

ENVIRONMENTAL AND SOCIAL RESPONSIBILITY

The concept of environmental and social responsibility in pineapple farming extends beyond mere compliance with regulations and certification standards. It involves a proactive commitment to minimizing negative impacts on the environment, conserving natural resources, and promoting the well-being of local communities.

Pineapple farms are encouraged to adopt sustainable agricultural practices that prioritize soil health, water conservation, and biodiversity preservation.

Environmental responsibility in pineapple farming may involve the implementation of integrated pest management strategies, precision agriculture techniques, and the use of renewable energy sources. Sustainable water management practices, such as rainwater harvesting and efficient irrigation systems, contribute to the conservation of water resources. Additionally, minimizing the carbon footprint through energy-efficient practices and responsible waste management aligns with the broader goal of environmental stewardship.

Social responsibility encompasses fair treatment of workers, community engagement, and support for local economies. Pineapple farms should prioritize safe working conditions, fair wages, and access to education and healthcare for their employees. Engaging with local communities through partnerships, employment opportunities, and community development projects fosters positive relationships and contributes to the overall well-being of the regions where pineapple farming takes place. By embracing environmental and social responsibility, pineapple farms can create a more sustainable and ethical industry, meeting the expectations of consumers and contributing to a healthier planet.

CHAPTER NINE

FUTURE TRENDS IN PINEAPPLE FARMING

TECHNOLOGICAL ADVANCES IN PINEAPPLE FARMING

In recent years, technological advances have significantly transformed the landscape of pineapple farming, enhancing efficiency and productivity. Precision agriculture, enabled by technologies such as GPS-guided tractors and drones, has revolutionized the way farmers manage their crops. These tools allow for precise monitoring of soil conditions, enabling farmers to optimize irrigation and fertilization practices. Additionally, sensor technologies embedded in the fields provide real-time data on plant health, helping farmers detect diseases or nutrient deficiencies early on.

Furthermore, the adoption of smart farming systems has become increasingly prevalent in pineapple cultivation.

These systems leverage the Internet of Things (IoT) to interconnect various devices and sensors throughout the farm. Farmers can remotely monitor and control irrigation, temperature, and humidity levels, ensuring optimal growing conditions. Automated machinery, equipped with artificial intelligence, aids in tasks such as harvesting and sorting, reducing labor costs and increasing overall efficiency in the pineapple farming process.

EMERGING MARKETS IN PINEAPPLE FARMING

Pineapple farming has witnessed a shift in focus towards emerging markets, driven by changing consumer preferences and global demand dynamics. As the middle class expands in developing regions, particularly in Asia and Africa, there is a growing appetite for tropical fruits like pineapples. This has prompted pineapple farmers to explore new markets and establish strategic partnerships to capitalize on the increasing demand.

Additionally, advancements in transportation and logistics have facilitated the export of pineapples to previously untapped regions. Improved cold-chain infrastructure ensures that pineapples can reach distant markets while maintaining freshness. As a result, pineapple farming is not only thriving in traditional strongholds like Central and South America but also gaining momentum in regions with burgeoning consumer markets.

SUSTAINABLE INNOVATIONS IN PINEAPPLE FARMING

Sustainability has become a focal point in modern agriculture, and pineapple farming is no exception. Farmers are adopting innovative practices to minimize environmental impact and promote long-term ecological balance. Agroecology, which emphasizes natural processes and biodiversity, has gained traction in pineapple cultivation. Integrated pest management, cover cropping, and organic fertilization methods are being implemented to reduce the reliance on synthetic chemicals.

Furthermore, sustainable packaging solutions are becoming a priority in the pineapple supply chain. Eco-friendly packaging materials and practices are being embraced to minimize waste and support environmentally conscious consumer choices. Some pineapple farms are also exploring renewable energy sources, such as solar power, to reduce their carbon footprint.

The future of pineapple farming is being shaped by technological advances, emerging markets, and sustainable innovations. As the industry continues to evolve, these trends will likely play a crucial role in ensuring the resilience and prosperity of pineapple cultivation on a global scale.